A strong affirmation is powerful and never to be undervalued or underestimated. The push most people really need in life begins with a word of encouragement that confirms they have what it takes to accomplish their goals. Begin your journey, today, as you absorb every page and every affirmation contained in this book.

CONTENTS

GIRL EMPOWERED
Affirmations for Pre-Teen And Teen Girls

Published by Verse One Enterprises
An imprint of E. Marcel Ministries

www.emarceljones.com

<u>GIRL EMPOWERED</u>
Affirmations for Pre-Teen/Teen Girls

Published by Verse One Enterprises
An imprint of E. Marcel Ministries

www.emarceljones.com

I AM
Loved

John 3:16

For God so loved the world that he gave his one and only Son, that whoever believes in him shall not perish but have eternal life.

You Are Loved

Plans for the week

Goals to achieve

Physical Challenge This Week

COMPLETE

- 5 PUSHUPS
- 10 SIT-UPS
- 20 JUMPING JACKS

What's On Your Mind?

WHO INFLUENCES ME THE MOST? WHY?

This Week...

TAKE A SELFIE OF YOURSELF HUGGING SOMEONE YOU LOVE

I AM

Respectful

Philippians 2:3

Do nothing from selfish ambition or conceit, but in humility count others more significant than yourselves.

You Are Respectful

Plans for the week

Goals to achieve

Physical Challenge This Week

COMPLETE

- 5 PUSHUPS

- 10 SIT-UPS

- 20 JUMPING JACKS

What's On Your Mind?

WHAT IS THE BEST COMPLIMENT I'VE EVER RECEIVED AND WHO GAVE IT TO ME?

This Week...

MAINTAIN A RESPECTFUL TONE AND PLEASANT ATTITUDE WHEN INTERACTING WITH OTHERS

I AM
Intelligent
Proverbs 18:15
An intelligent heart acquires knowledge, and the ear of the wise seeks knowledge.

You Are Intelligent

Plans for the week

Goals to achieve

Physical Challenge This Week

COMPLETE

- 5 PUSHUPS

- 10 SIT-UPS

- 20 JUMPING JACKS

What's On Your Mind?

MY FAVORITE SUBJECT IN SCHOOL IS... BECAUSE

This Week...

VISIT THE LIBRARY AND CHECK OUT A BOOK ON A SUBJECT ABOUT WHICH YOU KNOW VERY LITTLE

I AM
Strong
Ephesians 6:10
Finally, be strong in the Lord and in
the strength of his might.

You Are Strong

<table>
<tr><td>

Plans for the week

</td><td>

Goals to achieve

</td></tr>
</table>

Physical Challenge This Week

COMPLETE

- 7 PUSHUPS

- 20 SIT-UPS

- 30 JUMPING JACKS

What's On Your Mind?

THE STRONGEST PARTS OF MY BODY ARE MY...

This Week...

ADD FIVE MORE PUSHUPS, FIVE MORE SIT-UPS, AND FIVE MORE JUMPING JACKS TO YOUR EXERCISE ROUTINE

I AM
Wise

Proverbs 19:20

Listen to advice and accept instruction, that you may gain wisdom in the future.

You Are Wise

Plans for the week

Goals to achieve

Physical Challenge This Week

COMPLETE

- 7 PUSHUPS
- 20 SIT-UPS
- 30 JUMPING JACKS

What's On Your Mind?

THE BEST SHAPE THAT DESCRIBES MY PERSONALITY IS A _________ BECAUSE...

This Week...

BEFORE YOU MAKE A MAJOR DECISION, MAKE A LIST OF PROS AND CONS

I AM

Courageous

Proverbs 28:1

The wicked flee when no one pursues,
but the righteous are bold as a lion.

You Are Courageous

Plans for the week	Goals to achieve

Physical Challenge This Week

COMPLETE

- 7 PUSHUPS

- 20 SIT-UPS

- 30 JUMPING JACKS

What's On Your Mind?

THE MOST EMBARRASSING MOMENT I HAVE EVER EXPERIENCED WAS...

This Week...

CHALLENGE YOURSELF TO BE MORE COURAGEOUS WHEN YOU SPEAK

I AM

Luke 12:7

Why, even the hairs of your head are all numbered. Fear not; you are of more value than many sparrows.

You Are Needed

Plans for the week	Goals to achieve

Physical Challenge This Week

COMPLETE

- 10 PUSHUPS
- 25 SIT-UPS
- 35 JUMPING JACKS

What's On Your Mind?

THE MOST VALUABLE PART OF MY BODY... BECAUSE...

This Week...

CLEAN UP AN AREA OF THE HOUSE THAT HAS BEEN NEGLECTED

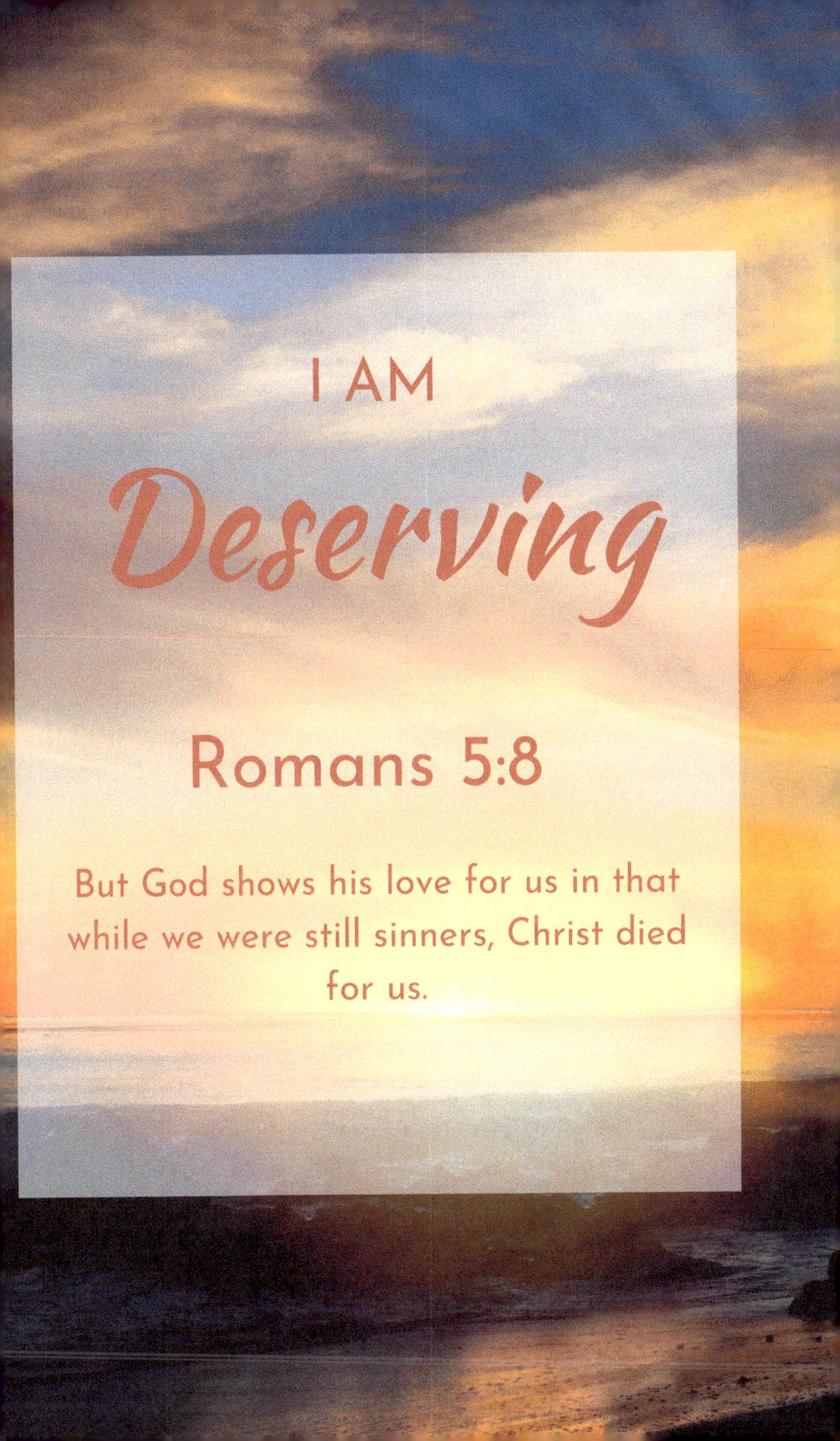

I AM

Deserving

Romans 5:8

But God shows his love for us in that
while we were still sinners, Christ died
for us.

You Are Deserving

<table>
<tr><td>**Plans for the week**</td><td>**Goals to achieve**</td></tr>
</table>

Physical Challenge This Week

COMPLETE

- 10 PUSHUPS

- 25 SIT-UPS

- 35 JUMPING JACKS

What's On Your Mind?

I WOULD SPEND A MILLION DOLLARS ON... BECAUSE...

This Week...

DO SOMETHING SPECIAL FOR YOURSELF (PREPARE YOUR FAVORITE MEAL, WATCH YOUR FAVORITE SHOW, ETC.)

I AM
Noble

Isaiah 32:8

But he who is noble plans noble things,
and on noble things he stands.

You Are Noble

Plans for the week

Goals to achieve

Physical Challenge This Week

COMPLETE

- 10 PUSHUPS

- 25 SIT-UPS

- 35 JUMPING JACKS

What's On Your Mind?

THE BEST SPORTS TEAM IS...

This Week...

ASSIST SOMEONE IN NEED OF A HELPING HAND

I AM
Persistent
Galatians 6:9
And let us not grow weary of doing good, for in due season we will reap, if we do not give up.

You Are Persistent

Plans for the week

Goals to achieve

Physical Challenge This Week

COMPLETE

- 10 PUSHUPS

- 25 SIT-UPS

- 35 JUMPING JACKS

What's On Your Mind?

THE TOUGHEST SUBJECT IN SCHOOL IS...
THE EASIEST SUBJECT IN SCHOOL IS...

This Week...

CHALLENGE YOURSELF TO COMPLETE A PERSONAL PROJECT, ASSIGNMENT, OR TASK

I AM
Reliable

Titus 2:7

Show yourself in all respects to be a
model of good works, and in your
teaching show integrity, dignity

You Are Reliable

Plans for the week	Goals to achieve

Physical Challenge This Week

COMPLETE

•STRETCH YOUR ARMS AND
LEGS FOR 10 MINUTES

What's On Your Mind?

HAS ANYONE EVER
DEPENDED ON ME? HOW?

This Week...

VOLUNTEER TO ASSIST YOUR TEACHER
OR PARENTS WITH A PROJECT

I AM

Beautiful

Genesis 1:27

So God created man in his own image,
in the image of God he created him;
male and female he created them.

You Are Beautiful

<table>
<tr><td>Plans for the week</td><td>Goals to achieve</td></tr>
</table>

Physical Challenge This Week

COMPLETE

- STRETCH YOUR ARMS AND LEGS FOR 15 MINUTES

What's On Your Mind?

WHAT I LIKE MOST ABOUT MY FACE IS...

This Week...

TAKE A SELFIE OF YOUR MOST BEAUTIFUL SMILE

I AM

Enough

I Corinthians 6:19

Or do you not know that your body is
a temple of the Holy Spirit within you,
whom you have from God? You are
not your own,

You Are Enough

<table>
<tr><td>Plans for the week</td><td>Goals to achieve</td></tr>
</table>

Physical Challenge This Week

COMPLETE

•STRETCH YOUR ARMS AND LEGS FOR 20 MINUTES

What's On Your Mind?

THE VALUES I PLAN TO TEACH MY CHILDREN ONE DAY ARE.. HERE'S WHY?

This Week...

REMIND YOURSELF DAILY THAT YOU ARE SMART ENOUGH, BEAUTIFUL ENOUGH, AND STRONG ENOUGH

I AM

I Corinthians 12:14

For the body does not consist of one member but of many.

You Are Important

Plans for the week	Goals to achieve

Physical Challenge This Week

COMPLETE

•TAKE A SLOW 10 MINUTE JOG
AROUND THE NEIGHBORHOOD
WITH A FAMILY MEMBER

What's On Your Mind?

MY TOP 3 HOBBIES ARE...

This Week...

DO SOMETHING SPECIAL FOR
YOURSELF EVERY DAY

I AM
Valuable

Matthew 10:29-31

Are not two sparrows sold for a penny? And not one of them will fall to the ground apart from your Father. But even the hairs of your head are all numbered. Fear not, therefore; you are of more value than many sparrows.

You Are Valuable

Plans for the week

Goals to achieve

Physical Challenge This Week

COMPLETE
•TAKE A SLOW 15 MINUTE JOG
AROUND THE NEIGHBORHOOD
WITH YOUR SIBLING

What's On Your Mind?

THE MOST EXPENSIVE
THING I OWN IS...

This Week...

REMIND YOURSELF DAILY THAT YOU
HAVE WORTH

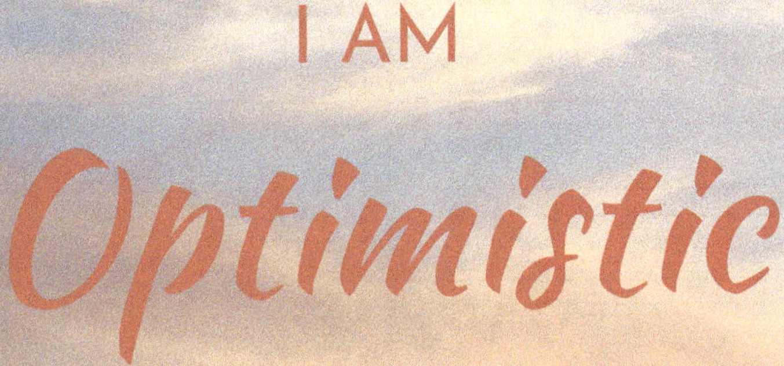

I AM
Optimistic
Jeremiah 29:11
For I know the plans I have for you,
declares the Lord, plans for welfare
and not for evil, to give you a future
and a hope.

You Are Optimistic

Plans for the week	Goals to achieve

Physical Challenge This Week

COMPLETE

•TAKE A SLOW 20 MINUTE JOG AROUND THE NEIGHBORHOOD WITH YOUR PARENT

What's On Your Mind?

THE BEST WAY TO SPEND THE WEEKEND IS...

This Week...

WRITE DOWN THREE THINGS YOU HOPE WILL HAPPEN BY THE END OF THE YEAR AND POST THEM ON YOUR MIRROR

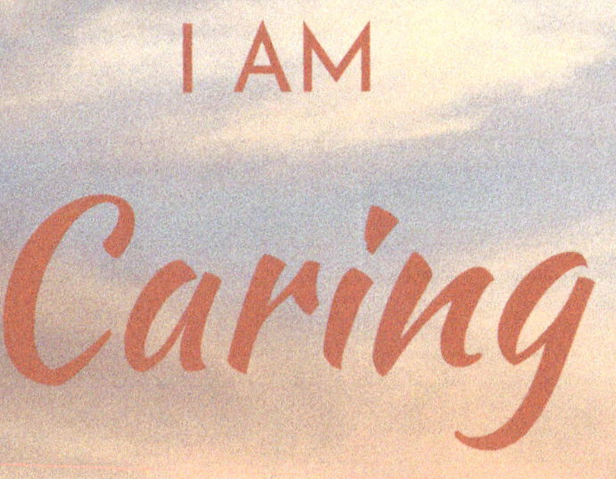

I AM
Caring

Colossians 3:12

Put on then, as God's chosen ones, holy and beloved, compassionate hearts, kindness, humility, meekness, and patience

You Are Caring

Plans for the week	Goals to achieve

Physical Challenge This Week

COMPLETE

•JUMP ROPE FOR 5 MINUTES

What's On Your Mind?

THE FIVE PEOPLE I CARE THE MOST ABOUT ARE..

This Week...

CONSIDER VOLUNTEERING AT A LOCAL CHARITY

I AM
Confident
Psalm 27:3
Though an army encamp against me,
my heart shall not fear;
though war arise against me,
yet I will be confident.

You Are Confident

Plans for the week	Goals to achieve

Physical Challenge This Week

COMPLETE

•JUMP ROPE FOR 7 MINUTES

What's On Your Mind?

MY BEST TALENT IS...

This Week...

TAKE A SELFIE THAT SHOWS OFF
YOUR MOST CONFIDENT LOOK

I AM

Motivated

I Corinthians 15:58

Therefore, my beloved brothers, be steadfast, immovable, always abounding in the work of the Lord, knowing that in the Lord your labor is not in vain.

You Are Motivated

Plans for the week	Goals to achieve

Physical Challenge This Week

COMPLETE

•JUMP ROPE FOR 8 MINUTES

What's On Your Mind?

ONE DAY, I PLAN TO TRAVEL TO... BECAUSE...

This Week...

SET YOUR ALARM FOR 30 MINUTES EARLIER
AND PRAY

I AM

Fearless

Isaiah 41:10

fear not, for I am with you;
be not dismayed, for I am your God;
I will strengthen you, I will help you, I
will uphold you with my righteous right
hand.

You Are Fearless

Plans for the week	Goals to achieve

Physical Challenge This Week

COMPLETE

• TAKE A 30 MINUTE WALK AROUND THE NEIGHBORHOOD

What's On Your Mind?

THESE THREE THINGS FRIGHTEN ME THE MOST...

This Week...

TAKE A SELFIE THAT SHOWS OFF YOUR MOST FEARLESS FACIAL EXPRESSION

I AM

Heroic

1 John 4:4

Little children, you are from God and have overcome them, for he who is in you is greater than he who is in the world.

You Are Heroic

Plans for the week

Goals to achieve

Physical Challenge This Week

COMPLETE

•TAKE A 30 MINUTE WALK
AROUND THE NEIGHBORHOOD

What's On Your Mind?

MY HERO IS... HERE'S WHY

This Week...

WRITE A THANK YOU LETTER TO A
LOCAL HERO AND MAIL OR EMAIL IT
TO HIM OR HER

I AM
Adventuresome

Colossians 3:23

Whatever you do, work heartily, as for
the Lord and not for men

You Are Adventuresome

Plans for the week	Goals to achieve

Physical Challenge This Week	What's On Your Mind?
COMPLETE •TAKE A 30 MINUTE WALK AROUND THE NEIGHBORHOOD	**MY FAVORITE CLOTHING ITEMS TO WEAR ARE...**

This Week...

ASK YOUR PARENTS TO TAKE YOU TO
A LOCAL MUSEUM

I AM
Determined

Philippians 4:13

I can do all things through him who strengthens me.

You Are Determined

Plans for the week

Goals to achieve

Physical Challenge This Week

COMPLETE

- 10 BURPEES
- 15 SQUATS
- 20 MOUNTAIN CLIMBERS

What's On Your Mind?

WHEN I BECOME AN ADULT, I PLAN TO MAKE A LIVING AS...

This Week...

WAKE UP DAILY WITH A DETERMINATION TO ACCOMPLISH SOMETHING GREAT

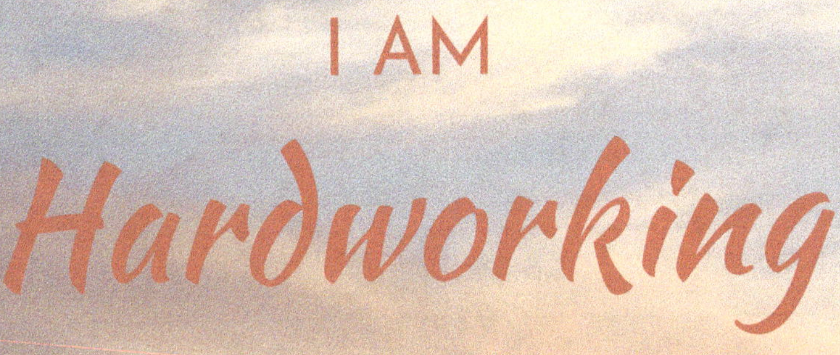

I AM
Hardworking
Proverbs 16:3
Commit your work to the Lord,
and your plans will be established.

You Are Hardworking

Plans for the week	Goals to achieve

Physical Challenge This Week

COMPLETE

- 10 BURPEES
- 15 SQUATS
- 20 MOUNTAIN CLIMBERS

What's On Your Mind?

WHAT DO I WISH I COULD CHANGE ABOUT THE WORLD THAT I LIVE IN?

This Week...

HELP YOUR PARENTS COMPLETE A TASK AROUND THE HOUSE

I AM

Galatians 6:9

And let us not grow weary of doing good, for in due season we will reap, if we do not give up.

You Are Diligent

Plans for the week

Goals to achieve

Physical Challenge This Week

COMPLETE

- 10 BURPEES
- 15 SQUATS
- 20 MOUNTAIN CLIMBERS

What's On Your Mind?

EVERY DAY, I NEED TO HEAR THESE FIVE (5) WORDS TO KEEP ME ENCOURAGED. WHY?

This Week...

PUT FORTH YOUR BEST EFFORT TO COMPLETE EVERY TASK YOU BEGIN

I AM

Successful

Genesis 39:2

The Lord was with Joseph, and he became a successful man, and he was in the house of his Egyptian master.

You Are Successful

Plans for the week	Goals to achieve

Physical Challenge This Week

COMPLETE

•5 PUSHUPS

•10 SIT-UPS

•20 JUMPING JACKS

What's On Your Mind?

I AM PROUD THAT I...

This Week...

LET YOUR PARENTS KNOW WHAT THINGS
YOU ACCOMPLISHED AT SCHOOL

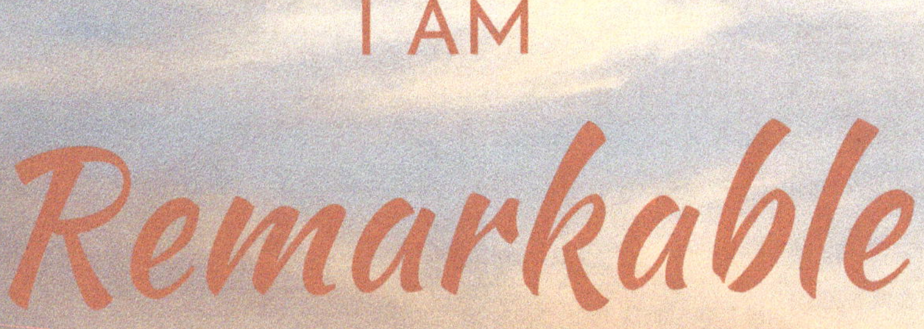

I AM

Remarkable

Psalm 139:14

I praise you, for I am fearfully and
wonderfully made.
Wonderful are your works;
my soul knows it very well.

You Are Remarkable

<table>
<tr><td>Plans for the week</td><td>Goals to achieve</td></tr>
</table>

Physical Challenge This Week

COMPLETE

- 5 PUSHUPS
- 10 SIT-UPS
- 20 JUMPING JACKS

What's On Your Mind?

WHAT MAKES ME UNIQUELY DIFFERENT FROM ANYONE ELSE?

This Week...

TAKE A SELFIE THAT SHOWS OFF YOUR BEST SMILE

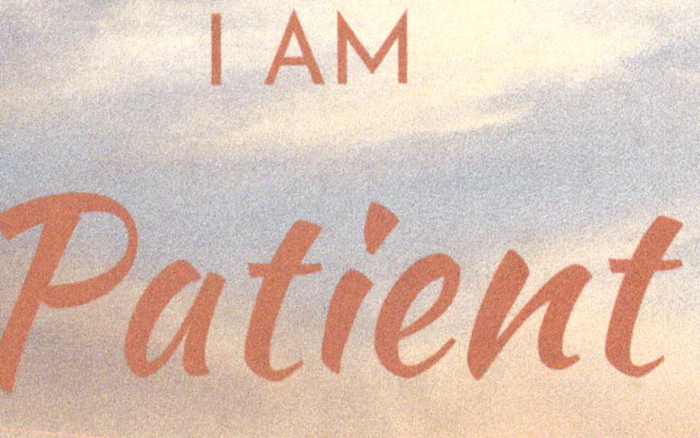

I AM
Patient
Isaiah 40:31
But they who wait for the Lord shall renew their strength; they shall mount up with wings like eagles; they shall run and not be weary; they shall walk and not faint.

You Are Patient

Plans for the week	Goals to achieve

Physical Challenge This Week

COMPLETE

- 5 PUSHUPS
- 10 SIT-UPS
- 20 JUMPING JACKS

What's On Your Mind?

IT'S HARD BEING PATIENT WHEN...

This Week...

EXERCISE A LITTLE MORE PATIENCE, DAILY, AS YOU INTERACT WITH OTHERS

I AM

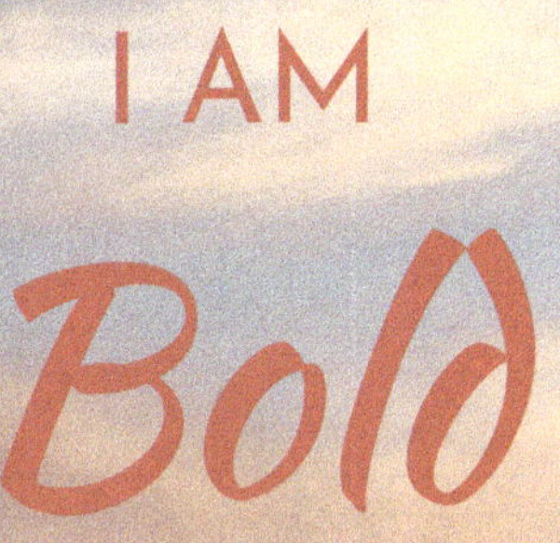

Deuteronomy 31:6

Be strong and courageous. Do not fear or be in dread of them, for it is the Lord your God who goes with you. He will not leave you or forsake you.

You Are Bold

Plans for the week	Goals to achieve

Physical Challenge This Week

COMPLETE

- 10 PUSHUPS
- 15 SIT-UPS
- 25 JUMPING JACKS

What's On Your Mind?

THE SCARIEST THING I EVER DID WAS...

This Week...

SPEAK OUT AGAINST ANY WRONGDOING THAT YOU WITNESS

I AM

Truthful

Colossians 3:9-10

Do not lie to one another, seeing that you have put off the old self with its practices and have put on the new self, which is being renewed in knowledge after the image of its creator.

You Are Truthful

<table>
<tr><th>Plans for the week</th><th>Goals to achieve</th></tr>
</table>

Physical Challenge This Week

COMPLETE

- 10 PUSHUPS
- 15 SIT-UPS
- 25 JUMPING JACKS

What's On Your Mind?

THE BEST ADVICE I'VE RECEIVED FROM MY PARENTS WAS...

This Week...

BE HONEST WHEN SOMEONE ASKS YOU TO SHARE YOUR THOUGHTS, BUT DO IT IN LOVE

I AM

Ambitious

I Timothy 6:11

But as for you, O man of God, flee these things. Pursue righteousness, godliness, faith, love, steadfastness, gentleness.

You Are Ambitious

<table>
<tr><td>Plans for the week</td><td>Goals to achieve</td></tr>
</table>

Physical Challenge This Week

COMPLETE

- 10 PUSHUPS
- 15 SIT-UPS
- 25 JUMPING JACKS

What's On Your Mind?

10 YEARS FROM NOW, I WILL BE...

This Week...

CREATE A FIVE-YEAR PLAN THAT HAS AT LEAST THREE PERSONAL GOALS TO ACHIEVE

I AM

Impressive

Ephesians 2:10

For we are his workmanship, created in Christ Jesus for good works, which God prepared beforehand, that we should walk in them.

You Are Impressive

Plans for the week	Goals to achieve

Physical Challenge This Week

COMPLETE

- 15 PUSHUPS
- 20 SIT-UPS
- 30 JUMPING JACKS

What's On Your Mind?

WHAT WILL MY REPORT CARD LOOK LIKE THIS PERIOD?

This Week...

DRESS UP ONE DAY JUST FOR THE FUN OF IT

I AM
Loyal
Proverbs 17:17
A friend loves at all times,
and a brother is born for adversity.

You Are Loyal

Plans for the week

Goals to achieve

Physical Challenge This Week

COMPLETE

- 15 PUSHUPS
- 20 SIT-UPS
- 30 JUMPING JACKS

What's On Your Mind?

THE TELEVISION SHOW I ENJOY THE MOST IS... BECAUSE...

This Week...

TEXT OR CALL YOUR BEST FRIEND AND WISH HIM OR HER A GREAT DAY

I AM
Unique

1 Peter 2:9

But you are a chosen race, a royal priesthood, a holy nation, a people for his own possession, that you may proclaim the excellencies of him who called you out of darkness into his marvelous light.

You Are Unique

Plans for the week

Goals to achieve

Physical Challenge This Week

COMPLETE

- 15 PUSHUPS
- 20 SIT-UPS
- 30 JUMPING JACKS

What's On Your Mind?

MOST PEOPLE DON'T KNOW THAT I...

This Week...

TAKE A SELFIE WEARING SOMETHING THAT MAKES YOU UNIQUE

I AM

Capable

Romans 8:31

What then shall we say to these things? If God is for us, who can be against us?

You Are Capable

Plans for the week

Goals to achieve

Physical Challenge This Week

COMPLETE

- 15 PUSHUPS
- 20 SIT-UPS
- 30 JUMPING JACKS

What's On Your Mind?

SOME PEOPLE THINK THIS IS DIFFICULT BUT IT COMES EASY TO ME...

This Week...

CHALLENGE YOURSELF TO BEGIN A NEW HOBBY

I AM
Creative

Exodus 35:35

He has filled them with skill to do every sort of work done by an engraver or by a designer or by an embroiderer in blue and purple and scarlet yarns and fine twined linen, or by a weaver—by any sort of workman or skilled designer.

You Are Creative

Plans for the week

Goals to achieve

Physical Challenge This Week

COMPLETE

- 10 BURPEES

- 15 SQUATS

- 20 MOUNTAIN CLIMBERS

What's On Your Mind?

THE MOST AWESOME THING I'VE EVER CREATED WAS...

This Week...

TAKE A PHOTO OF SOMETHING YOU CREATED ON YOUR OWN

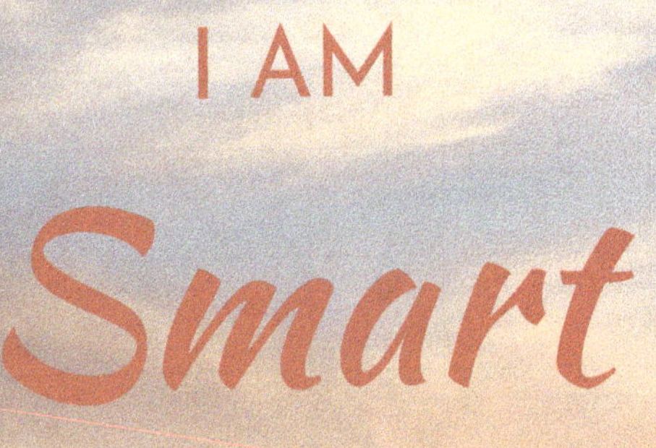

I AM

Smart

Proverbs 2:6

For the Lord gives wisdom;
from his mouth come knowledge
and understanding

You Are Smart

Plans for the week	Goals to achieve

Physical Challenge This Week

COMPLETE

- 10 BURPEES
- 15 SQUATS
- 20 MOUNTAIN CLIMBERS

What's On Your Mind?

I CONSTANTLY DREAM ABOUT...

This Week...

DEVELOP A SOLUTION TO A PROBLEM IN YOUR SCHOOL AND SUBMIT IT TO YOUR PRINCIPAL

I AM
Brilliant

2 Peter 1:5

For this very reason, make every effort to supplement your faith with virtue, and virtue with knowledge

You Are Brilliant

Plans for the week	Goals to achieve

Physical Challenge This Week

COMPLETE

- 10 BURPEES
- 15 SQUATS
- 20 MOUNTAIN CLIMBERS

What's On Your Mind?

ONE DAY, I WOULD LIKE TO MEET THIS FAMOUS PERSON...

This Week...

DEVELOP A PLAN THAT SOLVES AN ISSUE IN YOUR COMMUNITY AND PRESENT IT TO THE LOCAL NEWS STATION

I AM

Talented

Ephesians 2:10

For we are his workmanship, created in Christ Jesus for good works, which God prepared beforehand, that we should walk in them.

You Are Talented

<table>
<tr><td>Plans for the week</td><td>Goals to achieve</td></tr>
</table>

Physical Challenge This Week

COMPLETE

- 15 BURPEES
- 20 SQUATS
- 25 MOUNTAIN CLIMBERS

What's On Your Mind?

IF I HAD ONE SUPERHUMAN POWER, IT WOULD BE...

This Week...

MAKE A VIDEO THAT SHOWCASES YOUR BEST TALENT

I AM

2 Corinthians 8:8

I say this not as a command, but to prove by the earnestness of others that your love also is genuine.

You Are Genuine

<table>
<tr><td>Plans for the week</td><td>Goals to achieve</td></tr>
</table>

Physical Challenge This Week

COMPLETE
- 15 BURPEES
- 20 SQUATS
- 25 MOUNTAIN CLIMBERS

What's On Your Mind?

I CANNOT LIVE WITHOUT...
BECAUSE...

This Week...

COMPLIMENT YOUR FAVORITE TEACHER

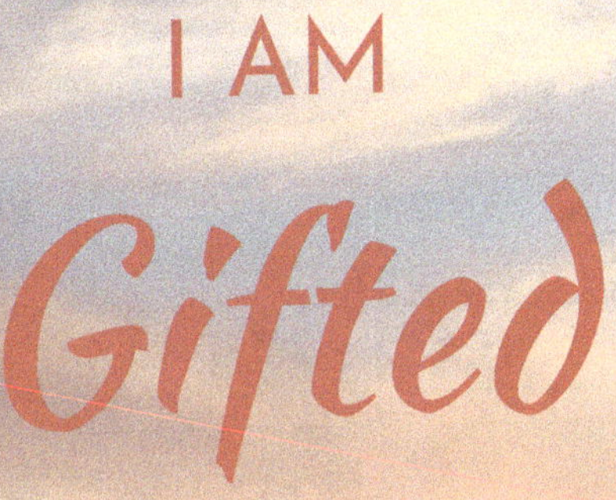

I AM

Gifted

1 Peter 4:10

As each has received a gift, use it to serve one another, as good stewards of God's varied grace:

You Are Gifted

Plans for the week

Goals to achieve

Physical Challenge This Week

COMPLETE

- 15 BURPEES
- 20 SQUATS
- 25 MOUNTAIN CLIMBERS

What's On Your Mind?

WHAT MOTIVATES ME TO BE GREAT?

This Week...

CREATE SOMETHING UNIQUE FROM A PIECE OF PAPER, SOME TAPE, AND A MARKER.

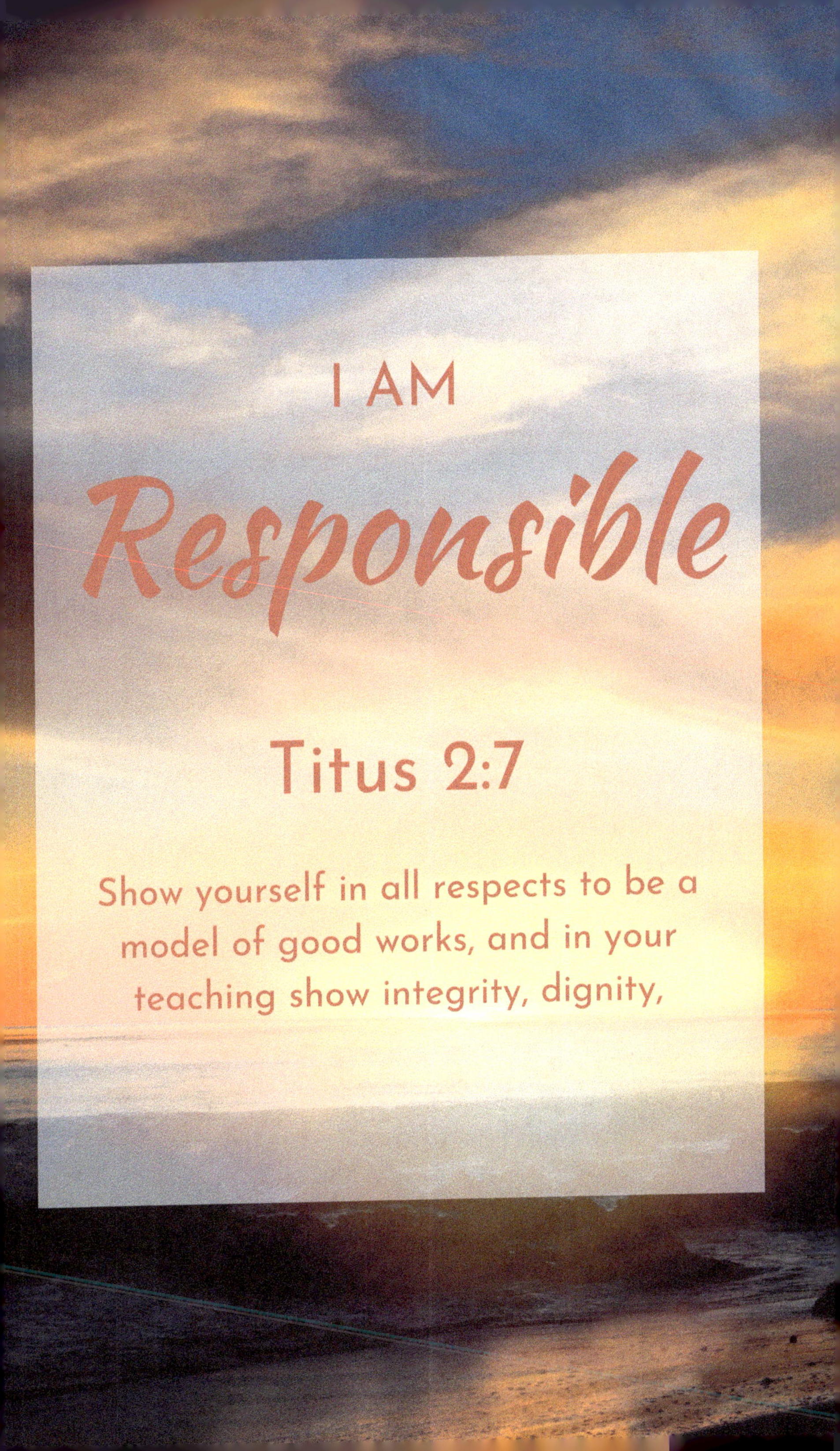

I AM

Responsible

Titus 2:7

Show yourself in all respects to be a model of good works, and in your teaching show integrity, dignity,

You Are Responsible

Plans for the week	Goals to achieve

Physical Challenge This Week

COMPLETE

A 20 MINUTE WALK AROUND THE NEIGHBORHOOD WITH A FRIEND OR FAMILY MEMBER

What's On Your Mind?

THESE THREE THINGS MAKE ME SMILE...

This Week...

COMPLETE A CHORE AROUND THE HOUSE BEFORE BEING ASKED TO DO IT

I AM

Devoted

Matthew 6:24

No one can serve two masters, for either he will hate the one and love the other, or he will be devoted to the one and despise the other. You cannot serve God and money.

You Are Devoted

<table>
<tr><td>Plans for the week</td><td>Goals to achieve</td></tr>
</table>

Physical Challenge This Week

COMPLETE

A 20 MINUTE WALK AROUND

THE NEIGHBORHOOD WITH A

FRIEND OR FAMILY MEMBER

What's On Your Mind?

MY BEST FRIEND'S NAME IS...

This Week...

READ ONE BIBLE VERSE EVERY NIGHT BEFORE BED

I AM
Competitive
I Corinthians 9:24
Do you not know that in a race all the runners run, but only one receives the prize? So run that you may obtain it.

You Are Competitive

Physical Challenge This Week

COMPLETE

A 25 MINUTE WALK AROUND

THE NEIGHBORHOOD WITH A

FRIEND OR FAMILY MEMBER

What's On Your Mind?

THE ONE SPORT THAT I'M
GOOD AT IS...

This Week...

CHALLENGE A FRIEND TO A GAME OF
UNO OR BOARD GAME OF YOUR CHOICE

I AM

Sincere

1 John 3:18

Little children, let us not love in word or talk but in deed and in truth.

You Are Sincere

Plans for the week	Goals to achieve

Physical Challenge This Week

COMPLETE

A 25 MINUTE WALK AROUND THE NEIGHBORHOOD WITH A FRIEND OR FAMILY MEMBER

What's On Your Mind?

MY FAVORITE TEACHER'S NAME IS...

This Week...

GIVE SOMEONE IN YOUR FAMILY A BIG MORNING HUG!

I AM

Innovative

Psalm 96:1

Oh sing to the Lord a new song;
sing to the Lord, all the earth!

You Are Innovative

Plans for the week	Goals to achieve

Physical Challenge This Week

COMPLETE

A 25 MINUTE WALK AROUND

THE NEIGHBORHOOD WITH A

FRIEND OR FAMILY MEMBER

What's On Your Mind?

MY MOST MEMORABLE
VACATION WAS...

This Week...

DRAW AN INVENTION THAT WOULD MAKE
LIFE EASIER FOR MILLIONS OF PEOPLE

I AM

Cooperative

Luke 6:31

And as you wish that others would do
to you, do so to them.

You Are Cooperative

Plans for the week

Goals to achieve

Physical Challenge This Week

COMPLETE

A 20 MINUTE WALK AROUND

THE NEIGHBORHOOD WITH A

FRIEND OR FAMILY MEMBER

What's On Your Mind?

THE TWO FOREIGN
LANGUAGES I WOULD
LOVE TO LEARN ARE...

This Week...

ASK SOMEONE IN YOUR FAMILY TO
HELP YOU COOK A MEAL

I AM

Friendly

John 15:12

This is my commandment, that you love one another as I have loved you.

You Are Friendly

Plans for the week

Goals to achieve

Physical Challenge This Week

COMPLETE

A 25 MINUTE WALK AROUND

THE NEIGHBORHOOD WITH A

FRIEND OR FAMILY MEMBER

What's On Your Mind?

WHO IS GOD TO ME?

This Week...

FIND TWO PEOPLE TO SHARE YOUR
SMILE WITH AND SAY A KIND WORD

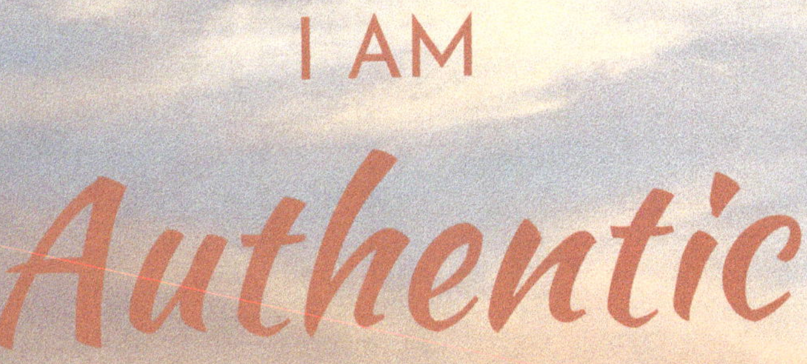

I AM
Authentic

Genesis 1:27

So God created man in his own image,
in the image of God he created him;
male and female he created them.

You Are Authentic

Plans for the week	Goals to achieve

Physical Challenge This Week

COMPLETE

A 25 MINUTE WALK AROUND THE NEIGHBORHOOD WITH A FRIEND OR FAMILY MEMBER

What's On Your Mind?

THESE SONGS MAKE ME DANCE LIKE NO ONE IS WATCHING ME?

This Week...

TEXT SOMEONE, "HAVE A GREAT DAY!"

I AM

Aspiring

Exodus 20:12

Honor your father and your mother,
that your days may be long in the land
that the Lord your God is giving you.

You Are Aspiring

Plans for the week

Goals to achieve

Physical Challenge This Week

COMPLETE

A 30 MINUTE WALK AROUND

THE NEIGHBORHOOD WITH A

FRIEND OR FAMILY MEMBER

What's On Your Mind?

ONE DAY, I WOULD LOVE
TO OWN THESE THREE
THINGS...

This Week...

POST A PICTURE OF WHAT YOU
WOULD LIKE TO BECOME AND TAPE IT
TO YOUR BEDROOM MIRROR

I AM

Focused

Colossians 3:2

Set your minds on things that are above, not on things that are on earth.

You Are Focused

Plans for the week	Goals to achieve

Physical Challenge This Week

COMPLETE

A 30 MINUTE WALK AROUND

THE NEIGHBORHOOD WITH A

FRIEND OR FAMILY MEMBER

What's On Your Mind?

THE WORST SCHOOL RULE
IS SCHOOL...

This Week...

WRITE DOWN YOUR TOP THREE GOALS FOR
THE YEAR AND POST THEM NEXT TO YOUR BED

I AM

Charitable

Acts 20:35

In all things I have shown you that by working hard in this way we must help the weak and remember the words of the Lord Jesus, how he himself said, "It is more blessed to give than to receive."

You Are Charitable

Plans for the week	Goals to achieve

Physical Challenge This Week

COMPLETE

A 30 MINUTE WALK AROUND THE NEIGHBORHOOD WITH A FRIEND OR FAMILY MEMBER

What's On Your Mind?

IF I STARTED A CHARITY IT WOULD BE FOR THE FOLLOWING CAUSE...

This Week...

COMPLETE THREE (3) ACTS OF KINDNESS

www.ingramcontent.com/pod-product-compliance
Lightning Source LLC
Chambersburg PA
CBHW071447030726
47593CB00003B/929